The Greatest Civil War Battles: The Second Battle of Bull Run (Second Manassas)

By Charles River Editors

THE SECOND BATTLE OF BULL RUN, FOUGHT AUG? 29TH 1862.

About Charles River Editors

Charles River Editors was founded by Harvard and MIT alumni to provide superior editing and original writing services, with the expertise to create digital content for publishers across a vast range of subject matter. In addition to providing original digital content for third party publishers, Charles River Editors republishes civilization's greatest literary works, bringing them to a new generation via ebooks.

Introduction

The Second Battle of Bull Run (Second Manassas)

"A splendid army almost demoralized, millions of public property given up or destroyed, thousands of lives of our best men sacrificed for no purpose. I dare not trust myself to speak of this commander as I feel and believe. Suffice to say...that more insolence, superciliousness, ignorance, and pretentiousness were never combined in one man." – Union II Corps Commander Alpheus Williams

The Second Battle of Bull Run (August 28-30, 1862) was one of the most decisive battles fought during the Civil War, and it was also one of the most unlikely. Less than three months before the battle, Joseph E. Johnston's Army of Northern Virginia had been pushed back nearly all the way to Richmond by George B. McClellan's Army of the Potomac, so close that Union soldiers could see the church steeples of the Confederate capital. And yet, at the end of Second Manassas, Robert E. Lee's Army of Northern Virginia found itself in the field unopposed about 20 miles away from the Union capital of Washington D.C. How could such a remarkable reversal of fortunes take place so quickly?

After Lee succeeded the wounded Johnston, he pushed McClellan's Army of the Potomac away from Richmond and back up the Peninsula in late June, only to then swing his army north to face a second Union army, John Pope's Army of Virginia. Needing to strike out before the Army of the Potomac successfully sailed back to Washington and linked up with Pope's army, Lee daringly split his army to threaten Pope's supply lines, forcing Pope to fall back to Manassas to protect his flank and maintain his lines of communication. At the same time, it left half of Lee's army (under Stonewall Jackson) potentially exposed against the larger Union army until the other wing (under James Longstreet) linked back up. Thus, in late August 1862, the Army of Northern Virginia and the Army of Virginia found themselves fighting over nearly the exact same land the South and North fought over in the First Battle of Bull Run 13 months earlier.

When Pope's army fell back to Manassas to confront Jackson, his wing of Lee's army dug in along a railroad trench and took a defensive stance. The battle began with the Union army throwing itself at Jackson the first two days. But the concentration on Stonewall's men opened up the Union army's left flank for Longstreet's wing, which marched 30 miles in 24 hours to reach the battlefield by the late afternoon of August 29. Lee used Longstreet's wing on August 30 to deliver a devastating flank attack before enough reinforcements from the retreating Army of the Potomac reached the field, sweeping Pope's Army from Manassas and forcing the Union soldiers into yet another disorderly retreat from Manassas to Washington D.C., a scene eerily reminiscent of the First Battle of Bull Run.

The Greatest Civil War Battles: The Second Battle of Bull Run comprehensively covers the campaign and the events that led up to the battle, the fighting itself, and the aftermath of the battle. Accounts of the battle by important participants are also included, along with maps of the battle and pictures of important people, places, and events. You will learn about the Second Battle of Bull Run like you never have before, in no time at all.

Ruins of the Stone Bridge at Bull Run after the battle.

Chapter 1: The Impact of the Peninsula Campaign

The Second Battle of Bull Run would be fought in late August about 25 miles outside of Washington D.C., but the Confederacy was facing a potential disaster around Richmond a few months earlier. The Union Army of the Potomac under "The Young Napoleon", George McClellan, had pushed the heavily outnumbered Army of Northern Virginia under Joseph Johnston to the outskirts of Richmond, seeking to capture the Confederate capital and possibly end the war.

During the Civil War, one of the tales that was often told among Confederate soldiers was that Joseph E. Johnston was a crack shot who was a better bird hunter than just about everyone else in the South. However, as the story went, Johnston would never take the shot when asked to, complaining that something was wrong with the situation that prevented him from being able to shoot the bird when it was time. The story is almost certainly apocryphal, used to demonstrate the Confederates' frustration with a man who everyone regarded as a capable general. Johnston began the Civil War as one of the senior commanders, leading (ironically) the Army of the Potomac to victory in the Battle of First Bull Run over Irvin McDowell's Union Army. But Johnston would become known more for losing by not winning. Johnston was never badly beaten in battle, but he had a habit of "strategically withdrawing" until he had nowhere else to go. Johnston continued to gradually pull his troops back to a line of defense nearer Richmond as McClellan advanced. In conjunction, the U.S. Navy began moving its operations further up the James River, until it could get within 7 miles of the Confederate capital before being opposed by a Southern fort. McClellan continued to attempt to turn Johnston's flank, until the two armies were facing each other along the Chickahominy River. McClellan's Army of the Potomac got close enough to Richmond that they could see the city's church steeples.

McClellan

By the end of May, Stonewall Jackson had startlingly defeated three separate Northern armies in the Valley, inducing Lincoln to hold back the I Corps from McClellan. When McClellan was forced to extend his line north to link up with troops that he expected to be sent overland to him, Johnston learned that McClellan was moving along the Chickahominy River. It was at this point that Johnston got uncharacteristically aggressive. Johnston had run out of breathing space for his army, and he believed McClellan was seeking to link up with McDowell's forces. Moreover, about a third of McClellan's army was south of the river, including Hancock's brigade in the IV Corps, while the other parts of the army were still north of it, offering Johnston an enticing target. Therefore he drew up a very complex plan of attack for different wings of his army, and struck at the Army of the Potomac at the Battle of Seven Pines on May 31, 1862.

Like McDowell's plan for First Bull Run, the plan proved too complicated for Johnston's army to execute, and after a day of bloody fighting little was accomplished from a technical standpoint. At one point during the Battle of Seven Pines, Confederates under General James Longstreet marched in the wrong direction down the wrong road, causing congestion and confusion among other Confederate units and ultimately weakening the effectiveness of the massive Confederate counterattack launched against McClellan.

By the time the fighting was finished, nearly 40,000 had been engaged on both sides, and it was the biggest battle in the Eastern theater to date (second only to Shiloh at the time). However, McClellan was rattled by the attack, and Johnston was seriously wounded during the fighting, resulting in military advisor Robert E. Lee being sent to assume command of the Army of Northern Virginia. McClellan confided to his wife, "I am tired of the sickening sight of the battlefield, with its mangled corpses & poor suffering wounded! Victory has no charms for me when purchased at such cost."

Lee

Although the Battle of Seven Pines was tactically inconclusive, McClellan's resolve to keep pushing forward vanished. He maneuvered his army so that it was all south of the Chickahominy, but as he settled in for an expected siege, Lee went about preparing Richmond's defenses and devising his own aggressive attacks.

From his first day in command, Lee faced a daunting, seemingly impossible challenge. McClellan had maneuvered nearly 100,000 troops to within seven miles of Richmond, three Union units were closing in on General Jackson's Confederates in Virginia's Shenandoah

Valley, and a fourth Union army was camped on the Rappahannock River ostensibly ready to come to McClellan's aid. On June 12, as McClellan sat on Richmond's eastern outskirts waiting for reinforcements, Lee began to ring the city with troop entrenchments.

However, with more Confederate troops swelling the ranks, Lee's army was McClellan's equal by late June, and on June 25, Lee commenced an all-out attempt to destroy McClellan's army in a series of fierce battles known as the Seven Days Battles. After a stalemate in the first fighting at Oak Grove, Lee's army kept pushing ahead, using Stonewall Jackson to attack McClellan's right. Although Stonewall Jackson was unusually lethargic during the week's fighting, the appearance of his "foot cavalry" spooked McClellan even more, and McClellan was now certain he was opposed by 200,000 men, more than double the actual size of Lee's army. It also made McClellan think that the Confederates were threatening his supply line, forcing him to shift his army toward the James River to draw supplies.

On June 26, the Union defenders sharply repulsed the Confederate attacks at Mechanicsville, in part due to the fact that Stonewall Jackson had his troops bivouac for the night despite the fact heavy gunfire indicating a large battle was popping off within earshot.

Stonewall Jackson

McClellan managed to keep his forces in tact (mostly through the efforts of his field generals), ultimately retreating to Harrison's Landing on the James River and establishing a new base of operation. Feeling increasingly at odds with his superiors, in a letter sent from Gaines' Mills, Virginia dated June 28, 1862, a frustrated McClellan wrote to Secretary of War Stanton, "If I save the army now, I tell you plainly that I owe no thanks to any other person in the Washington. You have done your best to sacrifice this army." McClellan's argument, however, flies in the face of common knowledge that he had become so obsessed with having sufficient supplies that he'd actually moved to Gaines' Mill to accommodate the massive amount of provisions he'd accumulated. Ultimately unable to move his cache of supplies as quickly as his men were needed, McClellan eventually ran railroad cars full of food and supplies into the Pamunkey River rather than leave them behind for the Confederates.

Despite the fact all of Lee's battle plans had been poorly executed by his generals, particularly Stonewall Jackson, he ordered one final assault against McClellan's army at Malvern Hill. Incredibly, McClellan was not even on the field for that battle, having left via steamboat back to Harrison's Landing. Biographer Ethan Rafuse notes McClellan's absence from the battlefield was inexcusable, literally leaving the Army of the Potomac leaderless during pitched battle, but McClellan often behaved coolly under fire, so it is likely not a question of McClellan's personal courage.

Ironically, Malvern Hill was one of the Union army's biggest successes during the Peninsula Campaign. Eventually, the Union artillery had silenced its Confederate counterparts, but there was then some miscommunication among the Confederate high command regarding whether or not the proposed assault should go forward. Lee abandoned his intention to assault, and Longstreet was informed, but those that didn't receive orders countermanding the assault went ahead with it, starting with D.H. Hill's division, which never got within 100 yards of the Union line. After the war, D.H. Hill famously referred to Malvern Hill, "It wasn't war. It was murder." Later that evening, as General Isaac Trimble (who is best known for leading a division during Pickett's Charge at Gettysburg) began moving his troops forward as if to attack, he was stopped by Stonewall Jackson, who asked "What are you going to do?" When Trimble replied that he was going to charge, Jackson countered, "General Hill has just tried with his entire division and been repulsed. I guess you'd better not try it."

After Malvern Hill, McClellan withdrew his army to Harrison's Landing, where it was protected by the U.S. Navy along the James River and had its flanks secured by the river itself. At this point, the bureaucratic bickering between McClellan and Washington D.C. started flaring up again, as McClellan refused to recommence an advance without reinforcements. After weeks of indecision, the Army of the Potomac was finally ordered to evacuate the Peninsula and link up with John Pope's army in northern Virginia, as the Administration was more comfortable having their forces fighting on one line instead of exterior lines. Upon his arrival in Washington, McClellan told reporters that his failure to defeat Lee in Virginia was due to Lincoln not sending sufficient reinforcements.

During the Seven Days Battles, Longstreet was more effective. In command of an entire wing of Lee's army, Longstreet aggressively attacked at Gaines' Mill and Glendale. Historians have credited Longstreet for those battles and criticized Stonewall Jackson for being unusually lethargic during the Seven Days Battles, ultimately contributing to Lee's inability to do more damage or capture McClellan's Army of the Potomac. Jackson's performance was not lost on

Longstreet, who pointed out that he performed poorly at the Seven Days Battles to defend charges that he was slow at Gettysburg. By the end of the campaign, Longstreet was one of the most popular and praised men in the army. Like Longstreet's father, Sorrel considered him a "rock in steadiness when sometimes in battle the world seemed flying to pieces." General Lee himself called Old Pete "the staff in my right hand." Though it is often forgotten, Longstreet was now Lee's principle subordinate, not Stonewall Jackson.

James Longstreet

Meanwhile, Porter Alexander, the artillery chief for Longstreet's corps, was extremely critical of Stonewall Jackson's lethargy, writing in his memoirs:

"This will be even more evident in the story of Jackson's column, now to be told. His command had always before acted alone and independently. Lee's instructions to him were very brief and general, in supreme confidence that the Jackson of the Valley would win even brighter laurels on the Chickahominy. The shortest route was assigned to him and the largest force was given him. Lee then took himself off to the farthest flank, as if generously to leave to Jackson the opportunity of the most brilliant victory of the war.

His failure is not so much a military as a psychological phenomenon. He did not try and fail. He simply made no effort. The story embraces two days. He spent the 29th in camp in disregard of Lee's instructions, and he spent the 30th in equal idleness at White Oak Swamp. His 25,000 infantry practically did not fire a shot in the two days."

At Richmond, Lee reorganized the Army of Northern Virginia into the structure it is best remembered by. Jackson now took command of a force consisting of his own division (now commanded by Brig. General Charles S. Winder) and those of Maj. General Richard S. Ewell,

Brig. General William H. C. Whiting, and Maj. General D. H. Hill. The other wing of Lee's army was commanded by Longstreet. On July 25, 1862, after the conclusion of the Seven Days Battles had brought the Peninsula Campaign to an end, JEB Stuart was promoted to Major General, his command upgraded to Cavalry Division, a promotion earned by his famous cavalry ride around McClellan's army earlier in the Peninsula Campaign.

JEB Stuart

Chapter 2: John Pope and the Army of Virginia

Lee and his army had pushed McClellan's Army of the Potomac away from Richmond, but there was little time for celebration in July 1862. While McClellan was trying to extricate his army from a tricky spot on the Virginian Peninsula, about 50,000 Union soldiers were menacing the Confederates in Northern Virginia, outnumbering Lee's army. If McClellan's Army of the Potomac linked up with the army now being gathered in Northern Virginia, they would vastly outnumber Lee and begin yet another drive toward Richmond. For Lee, the best option (and it was hardly a good one) was to try to prevent the two Union armies from linking up, and the only way to do that would be to inflict a decisive defeat upon the army in Northern Virginia before it was joined by McClellan's men.

Thus, even before McClellan had completely withdrawn his troops, Lee sent Jackson northward to intercept the new army President Abraham Lincoln had placed under Maj. General John Pope, which was formed out of the scattered troops in the Virginia area, including those who Stonewall Jackson had bedeviled during the Valley Campaign. Pope had successfully commanded Union soldiers in victories at Island No. 10 and during the Siege of Corinth, earning himself a promotion to Major General in March 1862.

However, Pope was also uncommonly brash, and he got off to a bad start with his own men by issuing one of the most notorious messages of the Civil War:

"Let us understand each other. I have come to you from the West, where we have always seen the backs of our enemies; from an army whose business it has been to seek the adversary and to beat him when he was found; whose policy has been attack and not defense. In but one instance has the enemy been able to place our Western armies in defensive attitude. I presume that I have been called here to pursue the same system and to lead you against the enemy. It is my purpose to do so, and that speedily. I am sure you long for an opportunity to win the distinction you are capable of achieving. That opportunity I shall endeavor to give you. Meantime I desire you to dismiss from your minds certain phrases, which I am sorry to find so much in vogue amongst you. I hear constantly of 'taking strong positions and holding them,' of 'lines of retreat,' and of 'bases of supplies.' Let us discard such ideas. The strongest position a soldier should desire to occupy is one from which he can most easily advance against the enemy. Let us study the probable lines of retreat of our opponents, and leave our own to take care of themselves. Let us look before us, and not behind. Success and glory are in the advance, disaster and shame lurk in the rear. Let us act on this understanding, and it is safe to predict that your banners shall be inscribed with many a glorious deed and that your names will be dear to your countrymen forever."

Pope

Pope's arrogance and patronization of soldiers in the Eastern theater turned off many of the men in his new command, and it even caught the notice of Lee, who uncharacteristically called his opponent a "miscreant".

Pope's Army of Virginia was officially consolidated on June 26, 1862, comprised of soldiers in various war departments who had been engaged in Northern Virginia earlier in the year. The army, about 50,000 strong, included three corps under Franz Sigel, Nathaniel Banks, and Irvin McDowell. Sigel replaced John Frémont, who outranked Pope and thus refused to be Pope's subordinate, while Banks had been bested in the Shenandoah Valley by Jackson and McDowell had lost the First Battle of Bull Run. Soldiers of the IX Corps under Ambrose Burnside, who would lead men disastrously at Antietam and Fredericksburg, would eventually link up with Pope's army ahead of the Second Battle of Bull Run

Each corps in Pope's army also had their own cavalry brigade, instead of centralizing the cavalry under one command, an organizational mistake that would not be fixed until after the battle. Conversely, Lee's cavalry were organized into one division under JEB Stuart and attached to Stonewall Jackson's wing of the Army of Northern Virginia. As a result of the Union army's organization, the smaller brigades of cavalry were both ineffective at traditional cavalry duties like screening the army's movements and performing reconnaissance, and their force was diluted in actual battle.

In addition to threatening Lee's army and Richmond, Pope's army was an immediate threat to the Virginian civilians in the area, and Pope's army began employing methods of appropriating resources that infuriated the Confederacy. Pope's General Order No. 5 instructed his men to "subsist upon the country," giving them the ability to take civilian supplies in exchange for vouchers that "loyal citizens of the United States" could turn in after the Civil War for reimbursement. General Orders 7 and 11 instructed soldiers to destroy any building that Confederate soldiers or partisans used to shoot at Union soldiers, and Pope also ordered his army to "arrest all disloyal male citizens within their lines or within their reach." While these policies were tame in comparison to the total warfare and scorched earth used in 1864 by William Tecumseh Sherman and Phil Sheridan, in the early years of the war they were still considered unconventional, and Lee was so incensed by them that he stated Pope "ought to be suppressed."

After the war, Pope would write about the campaign in a way that sought to defend his conduct, and he portrayed himself as far less arrogant in taking command of the Army of Virginia:

> "It became apparent to me at once that the duty to be assigned to me was in the nature
> of a forlorn-hope, and my position was still further embarrassed by the fact that I was
> called from another army and a different field of duty to command an army of which
> the corps commanders were all my seniors in rank. I therefore strongly urged that I be
> not placed in such a position, but be permitted to return to my command in the West, to

which I was greatly attached and with which I had been closely identified in several successful operations on the Mississippi. It was not difficult to forecast the delicate and embarrassing position in which I should be placed, nor the almost certainly disagreeable, if not unfortunate, issue of such organization for such a purpose.

It was equally natural that the subordinate officers and the enlisted men of those corps should have been ill-pleased at the seeming affront to their own officers, involved in calling an officer strange to them and to the country in which they were operating, and to the character of the service in which they were engaged, to supersede well-known and trusted officers who had been with them from the beginning, and whose reputation was so closely identified with their own. How far this feeling prevailed among them, and how it influenced their actions, if it did so at all, I am not able to tell."

Of course, if Pope had truly felt that way in 1862, it's unclear why he would have issued the patronizing message he had upon taking command.

Chapter 3: Cedar Mountain

Lee had taken a risk by sizing up McClellan and splitting his forces while the Army of the Potomac was still in the vicinity, but it was calculated and ultimately proved correct. With that, Lee decided upon trying to strike and hopefully destroy Pope's army before McClellan sailed his army back toward Washington D.C. However, shortly after sending Jackson north to take up a defensive stance against Pope near Gordonsville, Lee learned of intelligence suggesting Burnside's command was heading to unite with Pope, so he ordered A.P. Hill's 12,000 man "Light Division" to join Jackson. Despite the fact Lee now had only about 30,000 men at most opposing McClellan, the Union general continued to believe he was outnumbered and informed the Lincoln Administration he would need 50,000 more men to advance again. Then, despite having his request rejected and being given orders on August 3 to begin withdrawing his men from the Peninsula and head back to join Pope's army, McClellan protested before putting the withdrawal in motion on August 14.

McClellan has since been accused of intentionally delaying his evacuation out of spite and his disdain for Pope. McClellan was not in command at Second Bull Run, but he generated substantial controversy over whether he moved with speed to come to Pope's aid. What is unmistakable is that McClellan would feel vindicated if and when Pope was embarrassed, at one point mentioning that one possibility for the campaign is to let Pope attempt to get out of "his scrape." Lincoln would later accuse McClellan flat out of "acting badly" during the campaign.

On June 26, General Pope deployed his forces in an arc across Northern Virginia; its right flank (Sigel's corps) was around Sperryville on the Blue Ridge Mountains, the center consisted of Banks's corps at Little Washington, and its left flank (McDowell's corps) was outside Fredericksburg along the Rappahannock River. As Lee had anticipated, on August 6 Pope marched his forces south to capture the rail junction at Gordonsville, which meant to both threaten the Confederates from the north and distract Lee from McClellan's withdrawal from the Peninsula.

Just like in the Valley, Jackson's men were outnumbered by Pope's army, but Pope's corps were divided in three locations and none of them outnumbered Jackson individually. Jackson was thus determined to try to deal with them all separately before they could overwhelm him collectively.

Setting out on August 7, Jackson began marching his men toward the Union's isolated center, which consisted of about 8,000 men under Banks. However, his march was immediately hampered by a severe heat wave, which slowed his progress. On top of that, Jackson's insistence on keeping his marching plans secret messed up coordination among his principal subordinates, who were confused over which route they were supposed to take themselves. The delays allowed Pope to start shifting Sigel's corps to link up with Banks and form a defensive line around Cedar Run.

On August 9, Jackson's advancing column came into contact with the Union defenders posted on a ridge around Cedar Run, and they began forming a battle line while engaging in a general artillery duel with the Union forces. Jubal Early, whose brigade was in Jackson's vanguard, later explained, "No infantry had yet been seen, but the boldness with which the cavalry confronted us and the opening of the batteries, satisfied me that we had come upon a heavy force, concealed behind the ridge on which the cavalry was drawn up, as the ground beyond was depressed. I therefore halted the brigade, causing the men to cover themselves as well as they could by moving back a little and lying down, and then sent word for General Winder to come up."

However, the tempo of the battle changed on a dime after the mortal wounding of Confederate General Charles Winder, whose absence from the battlefield left the command of his division disorganized. A gap in the Confederate line opened up due to a misunderstanding by William Taliaferro, who had succeeded Winder, and that provided a chance for Banks to launch an attack. As Union soldiers came crashing down on the Confederates' right flank, another advance flanked the Confederates on their left and began rolling up their line.

Worried about losing control of his men and determined to inspire them, Jackson suddenly rode into the battlefield and attempted to brandish his sword, but the man who had once warned his VMI cadets to be ready to throw the scabbards of their swords away found that due to the infrequency with which he had used it, it had rusted in its scabbard. Waving his sword in its scabbard above his head, the Stonewall Brigade headed forward to reinforce the line.

However, the day wasn't saved for the Confederates until A.P. Hill's Light Division stabilized the Confederates' left flank and launched a counterattack. Jackson, who had not reconnoitered properly, was in danger of being beaten back by the vanguard of Banks's force when Hill came rushing in and changed the course of the battle, leading to a collapse of the Union right. Though outsiders thought Hill and Jackson worked like a "well oiled war machine," in reality, the two were maintaining an increasingly contentious relationship. The fact the two generals were at each other's throats was somewhat ironic, given that both of them were stern men. One of the men in his regiment recalled Hill's actions during the battle:

> "I saw A.P. Hill that day as he was putting his "Light Division" into battle, and was very much struck with his appearance. In his shirtsleeves and with drawn sword he sought to arrest the stragglers who were coming to the rear, and seeing a Lieutenant in the number, he rode at him and fiercely inquired: "Who are you, sir, and where are you going?" The trembling Lieutenant replied: "I am going back with my wounded friend." Hill reached down and tore the insignia of rank from his collar as he roughly said: "You are a pretty fellow to hold a commission -- deserting your colors in the presence of the enemy, and going to the rear with a man who is scarcely badly enough wounded to go himself. I reduce you to the ranks, sir, and if you do not go to the front and do your duty, I'll have you shot as soon as I can spare a file of men for the purpose." And then clearing the road, he hurried forward his men to the splendid service which was before them."

A.P. Hill

The Confederates had won the battle, but at a surprisingly staggering cost. Banks, who had attempted to take the offensive despite being outnumbered 2-1, lost over a quarter of his command, while Jackson had suffered nearly 1500 casualties himself. Jackson knew not to attempt the offensive anymore since Pope's army was beginning to link up, while the Lincoln Administration was ordering Pope to cancel his thrust towards Gordonsville.

Once certain McClellan was in full retreat, Lee began the process of reuniting his own army, still hoping to strike Pope before McClellan's troops could arrive as reinforcements. Lee wrote in his official post-campaign report:

"The victory at Cedar Run effectually checked the progress of the enemy for the time, but it soon became apparent that his army was being largely increased. The corps of Major-General Burnside from North Carolina, which had reached Fredericksburg, was reported to have moved up the Rappahannock a few days after the battle to unite with General Pope, and a part of General McClellan's army was believed to have left Westover for the same purpose. It therefore seemed that active operations on the James were no longer contemplated, and that the most effectual way to relieve Richmond from any danger of attack from that quarter would be to re-enforce General Jackson and advance upon General Pope.

Accordingly on August 13 Major-General Longstreet, with his division and the two brigades under General Hood, were ordered to proceed to Gordonsville. At the same time General Stuart was directed to move with the main body of his cavalry to that point, leaving a sufficient force to observe the enemy still remaining in Fredericksburg and to guard the railroad. General R. H. Anderson was also directed to leave his position on James River and follow Longstreet."

Meanwhile, Pope was apparently now convinced that he did not have enough strength to take the offensive, despite the fact his numbers were at least equal to the Army of Northern Virginia and he was being promised further reinforcements from Burnside's corps and McClellan's army. After the war, he wrote, "It is only necessary to say that the course of these operations made it plain enough that the Rappahannock was too far to the front, and that the movements of Lee were too rapid and those of McClellan too slow to make it possible, with the small force I had, to hold that line, or to keep open communication with Fredericksburg without being turned on my right flank by Lee's whole army and cut off altogether from Washington."

Lee was determined to attack Pope, Pope was being ordered to cancel his forward movements, and Pope was apparently of the mind that he had to take the defensive. The ball was now in Lee's court, and it would lead the two armies to very familiar ground.

Chapter 4: Moving Toward Manassas

Once Lee had united his army in mid-August, he was initially determined to try to slip around Pope's left flank, not his right. Lee explained in his post-campaign report:

"On the 16th the troops began to move from the vicinity of Gordonsville toward the

Rapidan, on the north side of which, extending along the Orange and Alexandria Railroad in the direction of Culpeper CourtHouse, the Federal Army lay in great force. It was determined with the cavalry to destroy the railroad bridge over the Rappahannock in rear of the enemy, while Longstreet and Jackson crossed the Rapidan and attacked his left flank. The movement, as explained in the accompanying order, was appointed for August 18, but the necessary preparations not having been completed, its execution was postponed to the 20th. In the interval the enemy, being apprised of our design, hastily retired beyond the Rappahannock. General Longstreet crossed the Rapidan at Raccoon Ford and, preceded by Fitzhugh Lee's cavalry brigade, arrived early in the afternoon near Kelly's Ford, on the Rappahannock, where Lee had a sharp and successful skirmish with the rear guard of the enemy, who held the north side of the river in strong force. Jackson passed the Rapidan at Somerville Ford and moved toward Brandy Station, Robertson's brigade of cavalry, accompanied by General Stuart in person, leading the advance. Near Brandy Station a large body of the enemy's cavalry was encountered, which was gallantly attacked and driven across the Rappahannock by Robertson's command."

Whether Lee's initial plan could have been successful if not for bad luck is unclear, but his plan was intercepted during a Union cavalry raid and brought to Pope, who used the news to withdraw to a tighter defensive line around the Rappahannock River. Rising waters made it far more dangerous for the Confederates to attempt to cross the Rappahannock with Union artillery on the other side of it. Moreover, Pope was biding his time in the hopes of receiving reinforcements from the Army of the Potomac that would greatly swing the numbers to the Union's advantage. He explained, "On the 21st of August, being then at Rappahannock Station, my little army confronted by nearly the whole force under General Lee, which had compelled the retreat of McClellan to Harrison's Landing, I was positively assured that two days more would see me largely enough reënforced by the Army of the Potomac to be not only secure, but to assume the offensive against Lee, and I was instructed to hold on "and fight like the devil."

Lee's next strategic shift was also a result of luck. Cavalry leader JEB Stuart had been concocting a plan to ride around Pope's army, just like he had done to McClellan's, only to be almost captured in the Union cavalry raid that had not only stolen Lee's orders but also one of his famous plumed hats. On August 22, Stuart's men conducted a raid on Pope's camp that bagged a bunch of valuables, as Longstreet explained in his memoirs:

"General Stuart was ordered over, with parts of his brigades, to investigate and make trouble in the enemy's rear. He crossed at Waterloo and Hunt's Mill with fifteen hundred troopers and Pelham's horse artillery, and rode to Warrenton. Passing through, he directed his ride towards Catlett's Station to first burn the bridge over Cedar Creek.

Before reaching Catlett's a severe storm burst upon him, bogging the roads and flooding the streams behind him. The heavy roads delayed his artillery so that it was after night when he approached Catlett's. He caught a picket-guard and got into a camp about General Pope's Headquarters, took a number of prisoners, some camp property, and, meeting an old acquaintance and friend in a colored man, who conducted him to General Pope's tents, he found one of the general's uniform coats, a hat, a number of official despatches, a large amount of United States currency, much of the general's personal equipments, and one of the members of his staff, Major Goulding. He made several attempts to fire the bridge near Catlett's, but the heavy rains put out all fires that could be started, when he sought axes to cut it away. By this time the troops about the camps rallied and opened severe fire against him, but with little damage. The heavy rainfall admonished him to forego further operations and return to the army while yet there was a chance to cross Cedar Creek and the Rappahannock before the tides came down. On the night of the 23d he reached Sulphur Springs, where he met General Jackson's troops trying to make comfortable lodgement on the east bank, passed over, and resumed position outside General Lee's left. The despatch-book of General Pope gave information of his troops and his anxiety for reinforcements, besides mention of those that had joined him, but General Stuart's especial pleasure and pride were manifested over the possession of the uniform coat and hat of General Pope. Stuart rode along the line showing them, and proclaiming that he was satisfied with the exchange that made even his loss at Verdierville before the march; but the despatch lost at Verdierville [Lee's orders] was the tremendous blow that could not be overestimated."

With information about Pope's dispositions, his strategic thinking, and the news about impending reinforcements, Lee now changed tack and decided to try to turn Pope's right, as he explained in his report:

"As our positions on the south bank of the Rappahannock were commanded by those of the enemy, who guarded all the fords, it was determined to seek a more favorable place to cross higher up the river, and thus gain the enemy's right. Accordingly, General Longstreet was directed to leave Kelly's Ford on the 21st and take the position in front of the enemy in the vicinity of Beverly Ford and the Orange and Alexandria Railroad bridge, then held by Jackson, in order to mask the movement of the latter, who was instructed to ascend the river.

On the 22d Jackson crossed Hazel River at Welford's Mill and proceeded up the Rappahannock, leaving Trimble's brigade near Freeman's Ford to protect his trains. In the afternoon Longstreet sent General Hood, with his own and Whiting's brigade, under Colonel Law, to relieve Trimble. Hood had just reached the position when he and Trimble were attacked by a considerable force which had crossed at Freeman's Ford. After a short but spirited engagement the enemy was driven precipitately over the river with heavy loss. General Jackson arrived at the Warrenton Springs Ford in the afternoon, and immediately began to cross his troops to the north side, occupying the

Springs and the adjacent heights. He was interrupted by a heavy rain, which caused the river to rise so rapidly that the ford soon became impassable for infantry and artillery."

While Lee was sending Jackson stealthily past Pope's right, the two armies skirmished around the Rappahannock River from August 22-25, which preoccupied Pope and helped keep his army in place and vulnerable to Jackson's turning movement. Meanwhile, Jackson's wing of the Army of Northern Virginia was heading toward Bristoe Station and the railroad junction at Manassas, where he would be positioned not only to destroy Pope's supply lines but also potentially cut off Pope's line of retreat.

Pope learned about Jackson's turning movement on August 26, and his initial response was to try to coordinate the dispositions of the reinforcements he thought he was due to receive imminently:

"I accordingly held on till the 26th of August, when, finding myself to be outflanked on my right by the main body of Lee's army, while Jackson's corps having passed Salem and Rectortown the day before were in rapid march in the direction of Gainesville and Manassas Junction, and seeing that none of the reënforcements promised me were likely to arrive, I determined to abandon the line of the Rappahannock and communications with Fredericksburg, and concentrate my whole force in the direction of Warrenton and Gainesville, to cover the Warrenton pike, and still to confront the enemy rapidly marching to my right.^

Stonewall Jackson's movement on Manassas Junction was plainly seen and promptly reported, and I notified General Halleck of it. He informed me on the 23d of August that heavy reënforcements would begin to arrive at Warrenton Junction on the next day (24th), and as my orders still held me to the Rappahannock I naturally supposed that these troops would be hurried forward to me with all speed. Franklin's corps especially, I asked, should be sent rapidly to Gainesville. I also telegraphed Colonel Herman Haupt, chief of railway transportation, to direct one of the strongest divisions coming forward, and to be at Warrenton Junction on the 24th, to be put in the works at Manassas Junction. A cavalry force had been sent forward to observe the Thoroughfare Gap early on the morning of the 26th, but nothing was heard from it."

By the time Pope was aware of Jackson's move on his right, the Confederates were well into his rear. On the night of August 26, Jackson's men slipped through Thoroughfare Gap and headed for the railroad at Bristoe Station, cutting up the line. The following morning, Jackson moved on the Union supplies stored at Manassas Junction, where he met one sole Union brigade led by George W. Taylor and easily pushed it aside, mortally wounding Taylor in the process. McClellan would later cite the defeat of Taylor's force as justification for not sending more infantry reinforcements to Pope without corresponding artillery and cavalry for their protection.

However, by the end of August 27, Jackson's men were being chased by a Union division under the command of "Fighting Joe" Hooker, forcing Jackson to conduct a rearguard action while he retreated and dug in behind an unfinished railroad near Bull Run creek. Jackson had posted his men about a mile away from where he had become a Confederate hero the year before during First Manassas, when his brigade had rallied the Confederates on Henry Hill and turned the tide of that battle. Now he was digging in right on a spot that Union soldiers opposing him had stood on 13 months earlier. Lee later reported, "General Jackson's force being much inferior to that of General Pope, it became necessary for him to withdraw from Manassas and take a position west of the turnpike road from Warrenton to Alexandria, where he could more readily unite with the approaching column of Longstreet. Having fully supplied the wants of his troops, he was compelled, for want of transportation, to destroy the rest of the captured property. This was done during the night of the 27th, and 50,000 pounds of bacon, 1,000 barrels of corned beef, 2,000 barrels of salt pork, and 2,000 barrels of flour, besides other property of great value, were burned."

On August 27, Jackson routed a Union brigade near Union Mills (Bull Run Bridge), inflicting several hundred casualties and mortally wounding Union Brig. Gen. George W. Taylor. Maj. Gen. Richard S. Ewell's Confederate division fought a brisk rearguard action against Maj. Gen. Joseph Hooker's Union division at Kettle Run, resulting in about 600 casualties. Ewell held back Union forces until dark. That night, Jackson marched his divisions north to the Bull Run battlefield, where he took position behind an unfinished railroad grade. Pope explained the outlook on the night of August 27, "The movement of Jackson presented the only opportunity which had offered to gain any success over the superior forces of the enemy. I determined, therefore, on the morning of the 27th of August to abandon the line of the Rappahannock and throw my whole force in the direction of Gainesville and Manassas Junction, to crush any force of the enemy that had passed through Thoroughfare Gap, and to interpose between Lee's army and Bull Run. Having the interior line of operations, and the enemy at Manassas being inferior in force, it appeared to me, and still so appears, that with even ordinary promptness and energy we might feel sure of success."

Picture of a train derailed near Manassas Junction by the raiding Confederates

With the Confederate army divided and Pope's army inbetween them, Pope was now positioned to prevent them from linking up by blocking the Thoroughfare Gap. Ultimately he opted not to, later claiming that when he saw smoke from the flames shooting near Manassas, he figured he had Jackson in trouble and could annihilate the Confederates before Longstreet reunited with them. In fact, those flames were coming from his own supplies, after Jackson's men began torching what they couldn't carry. As a result, Longstreet's wing of the army would suffer only a slight harassment from Union cavalry and one Union division before they gave way at Thoroughfare Gap.

With the path established for Longstreet's wing to march and reunite with Jackson's wing, the race was now on. Could Pope's army fall on Jackson's wing and destroy it before Longstreet rejoined it?

Chapter 5: August 28

Although Pope was now planning to thrust at Jackson's army, the Second Battle of Bull Run actually began on the evening of August 28 with Jackson's men taking the offensive. Pope was in the process of gathering all his men at Centreville, just above Bull Run and a few miles away from Jackson's men, because he thought Jackson's men were at Centreville itself. As Jackson's men kept their defensive line along the unfinished railroad cut, they watched a Union column marching along the Warrenton Turnpike near Brawner's farm, and it turned out to be soldiers from Brig. Gen. Rufus King's division (of McDowell's corps) marching toward Centreville to meet up with the rest of Pope's army and hopefully discover Jackson. Unbeknownst to the column, they were actually marching right past Jackson's entire wing of the army.

Emboldened by the news that Longstreet was passing through Thoroughfare Gap around the same time, Jackson got characteristically aggressive, and figuring that this Union column was retreating behind Bull Run to link up with Pope's army and perhaps even reinforcements from the Army of the Potomac, he decided to try to annihilate the column.

In the late afternoon, Jackson ordered his principal officers, "Bring out your men, gentlemen." With that, he ordered his artillery to open up on the column marching conspicuously across their front. As fate would have it, the part of the column in Jackson's front at this time was John Gibbon's brigade, which could be identified by their Black Hats. This "Black Hat Brigade" was destined to become one of the most famous Union brigades of the war after being christened the Iron Brigade by McClellan during the subsequent Maryland Campaign and fighting heroically at Gettysburg, but they had never seen action before Jackson's grizzled veterans opened fire on them that night around 6:30 p.m.

John Hatch's brigade of King's division had already marched past Jackson's front, so Gibbon worked to get reinforcements from Abner Doubleday's brigade and formed a battle line. Due to Pope's belief that Jackson was at Centreville, Gibbon mistakenly thought that the artillery being fired at them was coming from JEB Stuart's cavalry, and that two brigades could sweep them aside and end the harassment of their march. The Black Hat Brigade had never fought before, and now they were about to make a general advance against half of the Army of Northern Virginia.

Gibbon

While Gibbon formed his line along the turnpike, he used the 2nd Wisconsin regiment to advance through woods on the Confederates' right flank. In fact, when Gibbon convened with the regiment in the woods, he instructed them to capture the artillery. In reality, he was posting a lone regiment on the right flank of Richard S. Ewell's entire division, which was supported in the rear by William Taliaferro's division.

With his line formed, Gibbon's previously untested men began moving forward, only to come face to face with Confederates at nearly point blank range in Brawner's farm. Major Rufus Dawes, who would become a hero on Day 1 at Gettysburg in command of the 6th Wisconsin, described the fighting the 6th Wisconsin endured that night, "Our men on the left loaded and fired with the energy of madmen, and the 6th worked with equal desperation. This stopped the rush of the enemy and they halted and fired upon us their deadly musketry. During a few awful moments, I could see by the lurid light of the powder flashes, the whole of both lines. The two ...

were within ... fifty yards of each other pouring musketry into each other as fast as men could load and shoot."

Meanwhile, the 2nd Wisconsin came through the woods and found themselves squarely on the Confederates' right flank at an angle that also happened to expose their own right flank. Thankfully for the Union, the 2nd Wisconsin was one of the few veteran regiments on the field that night, and they stood firm even after the Stonewall Brigade unleashed the first volley, firing a volley of their own and thus starting a general musketry exchange. Out of the nearly 430 men fighting for the 2nd Wisconsin, nearly 60% would become casualties.

The fact that daylight was running out likely contributed to the confusion that induced Gibbon to stand firm against the artillery assault, but it would also prove to be his saving grace. Gibbon shored up the right of his line with men from Doubleday's brigade and kept plugging in gaps in his line, and the fighting was so hot that Jackson actually started directing single regiments into the fighting. While Jackson was ordering multiple regiments into the fray, the unwitting Gibbon was countering by ordering up single regiments. Jackson described the fighting, "In a few moments our entire line was engaged in a fierce and sanguinary struggle with the enemy. As one line was repulsed another took its place and pressed forward as if determined by force of numbers and fury of assault to drive us from our positions."

By the time Jackson ordered up Isaac Trimble's brigade, it was so dark that all semblance of command coordination vanished. The Confederates started making piecemeal assaults instead of a general advance, allowing the heavily outnumbered Union regiments to repulse the attacks one at a time. By 9:00, the Union soldiers fought a gradual retreat back to the turnpike, leaving the field to Jackson's men. The fighting had produced a remarkable number of casualties in just 2 hours, with 1,150 Union and 1,250 Confederate casualties. Nevertheless, the Union soldiers had held their ground despite being outnumbered 3-1, and furthermore the Confederate casualties included Ewell and Taliaferro, two of Jackson's division commanders.

Ewell

Pope later wrote about where he was and what he was thinking when he heard about the fighting on the night of the 28th.

"The engagement of King's division was reported to me about 10 o'clock at night near Centreville. I felt sure then, and so stated, that there was no escape for Jackson. On the west of him were McDowell's corps (I did not then know that he had detached Ricketts *, Sigel's corps, and Reynolds's division, all under command of McDowell. On the east of him, and with the advance of Kearny nearly in contact with him on the Warrenton pike, were the corps of Reno and Heintzelman. Porter was supposed to be at Manassas Junction, where he ought to have been on that afternoon.

"I sent orders to McDowell (supposing him to be with his command), and also direct to General King, several times during that night and once by his own staff-officer, to hold his ground at all hazards, to prevent the retreat of Jackson toward Lee, and that at daylight our whole force from Centreville and Manassas would assail him from the east, and he would be crushed between us. I sent orders also to General Kearny at Centreville to move forward cautiously that night along the Warrenton pike; to drive in the pickets of the enemy, and to keep as closely as possible in contact with him during the night, resting his left on the Warrenton pike and throwing his right to the north, if practicable, as far as the Little River pike, and at daylight next morning to assault vigorously with his right advance, and that Hooker and Reno would certainly be with him shortly after daylight. I sent orders to General Porter, who I supposed was at Manassas Junction, to move upon Centreville at dawn, stating to him the position of our forces, and that a severe battle would be fought that morning (the 29th).

With Jackson at or near Groveton, with McDowell on the west, and the rest of the army on the east of him, while Lee, with the mass of his army, was still west of Thoroughfare Gap, the situation for us was certainly as favorable as the most sanguine person could desire, and the prospect of crushing Jackson, sandwiched between such forces, were certainly excellent. There is no doubt, had General McDowell been with his command when King's division of his corps became engaged with the enemy, he would have brought forward to its support both Sigel and Reynolds, and the result would have been to hold the ground west of Jackson at least until morning brought against him also the forces moving from the direction of Centreville.

To my great disappointment and surprise, however, I learned toward daylight the next morning (the 29th) that King's division had fallen back toward Manassas Junction, and that neither Sigel nor Reynolds had been engaged or had gone to the support of King. The route toward Thoroughfare Gap had thus been left open by the wholly unexpected retreat of King's division, due to the fact that he was not supported by Sigel and Reynolds, and an immediate change was necessary in the disposition of the troops under my command."

However, as Longstreet noted in his memoirs, Pope actually had it backwards. Longstreet's wing of the army was already on its way through Thoroughfare Gap after pushing aside relatively light resistance, and Jackson's men could actually see the musket smoke and hear the artillery produced by Longstreet's soldiers in the Gap. Longstreet wrote, "During the night the Federal commander reported to his subordinates that McDowell had 'intercepted the retreat of Jackson, and ordered concentration of the army against him,' whereas it was, of course, Jackson who had intercepted McDowell's march. He seems to have been under the impression that he was about to capture Jackson, and inclined to lead his subordinates to the same opinion."

Sure enough, Pope was operating under the mistaken assumption that Jackson's men had engaged King's division as it was retreating from Centreville, clearly unaware that Jackson had taken up that position the night before and was biding his time until Longstreet joined him. That night, Pope told Phil Kearny, who commanded a division in the Army of the Potomac, "General McDowell has intercepted the retreat of the enemy and is now in his front ... Unless he can escape by by-paths leading to the north to-night, he must be captured." In actuality, when King's division extricated itself from the fighting at Brawner's farm and continued east to meet up with the rest of Pope's army, there were no longer any Union forces between Jackson and Longstreet.

Chapter 6: August 29

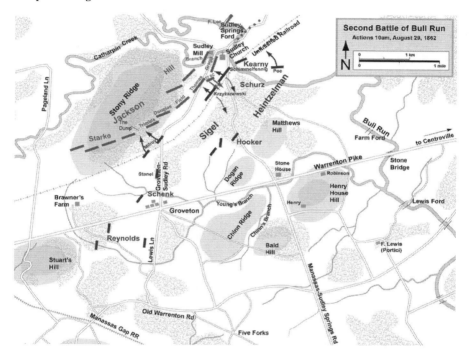

The battle lines on the morning of August 29

Pope would begin operations on August 29 laboring under an entirely faulty premise, and his various orders to different subordinates would result in a completely uncoordinated general attack on Jackson's defensive line.

"About daylight, therefore, on the 29th of August, almost immediately after I received information of the withdrawal of King's division toward Manassas Junction, I sent orders to General Sigel, in the vicinity of Groveton, to attack the enemy vigorously at daylight and bring him to a stand if possible. He was to be supported by Reynolds's division. I instructed Heintzelman to push forward from Centreville toward Gainesville on the Warrenton pike at the earliest dawn with the divisions of Kearny and Hooker, and gave orders also to Reno with his corps to follow closely in their rear. They were directed to use all speed, and as soon as they came up with the enemy to establish communication with Sigel, and to attack vigorously and promptly. I also sent orders to General Porter at Manassas Junction to move forward rapidly with his own corps and King's division of McDowell's corps, which was there also, upon Gainesville by the direct route from Manassas Junction to that place. I urged him to make all possible speed, with the purpose that he should come up with the enemy or connect himself with the left of our line near where the Warrenton pike is crossed by the road from Manassas Junction to Gainesville.

Shortly after sending this order I received a note from General McDowell, whom I had not been able to find during the night of the 28th, dated Manassas Junction, requesting that King's division be not taken from his command. I immediately sent a joint order, addressed to Generals McDowell and Porter, repeating the instructions to move forward with their commands toward Gainesville, and informing them of the position and movements of Sigel and Heintzelman."

Heintzelman

Thus, with Longstreet marching his 26,000 soldiers toward Jackson at dawn that morning, it would fall upon Jackson and his nearly 20,000 men to hold out for at least the entire morning against potentially all of Pope's army.

Luckily for the Confederates, Pope's unfamiliarity with the Confederate dispositions and his convoluted attack orders would ruin his plans. Pope intended to strike both of Jackson's flanks that morning, and Sigel began the fighting around 7:00 a.m. on Jackson's left with Robert Schenck's division, Carl Schurz's division, and Robert Milroy's brigade. His line also had John Reynolds's division from Heintzelman's corps in reserve, and he anticipated being supported by Kearny's division as well.

Sigel advanced his men without knowing exactly where Jackson's flank was, and as it turned out A.P. Hill had extended Jackson's left until it was nearly touching Bull Run creek, and Stuart's cavalry was posted on the other side of the creek crossing to provide artillery support. While Stuart's horse artillery was engaged, the cavalrymen fastened logs and dragged them on the dirt road behind their horses, kicking up a cloud of dust that was meant to confuse Union commanders into thinking Jackson had more men than he actually did.

Franz Sigel

For the next three hours, Sigel threw his corps at A.P. Hill's Light Division in a series of attacks that were not properly coordinated with the supporting elements from the other corps of the army. At the same time, even though Jackson was essentially fighting a delaying action intended to buy time for Longstreet, Hill's men couldn't help but charge forward and counterattack Sigel's men after repulsing each attack. In addition to Sigel's divisions fighting piecemeal, those divisions had their brigades fighting piecemeal. Making matters worse, Sigel made one last assault around 10:00 a.m. in the belief that Phil Kearny's division was making the attack with them. To Sigel's horror, Kearny's division didn't move as he had expected. Historians have attributed Kearny's failure to move for his disdain for Sigel, but Kearny insisted in his post-battle report, "On the 29th, on my arrival, I was assigned to the holding of the right wing, my left on Leesburg road. I posted Colonel Poe, with Berry's brigade, in first line, General Robinson, First Brigade, on his right, partly in line and partly in support, and kept Birney's most disciplined regiments reserved and ready for emergencies. Toward noon I was obliged to occupy a quarter of a mile additional on left of said road, from Schurz' troops being taken elsewhere."

Despite being repulsed, Pope wasn't done attacking Jackson's left. Hooker's division (from Heintzelman's corps) now came up, as did a brigade from Burnside's IX Corps led by Isaac Stevens. Kearny's division was also still ready to make an assault on the left. Pope arrived at the scene around noon, just in time to watch this next wave of attacks on Jackson's left.

As those attacks were starting, the first elements of Longstreet's wing were coming up on Jackson's right, as were some of Stuart's cavalry, which had been employed in guiding Longstreet's men to Jackson's line. As Longstreet's men began arriving, Longstreet recounted an exchange between he and Lee over whether to conduct an attack on Pope's left flank, which was at that time was concentrating its efforts on Jackson: "When I reported my troops in order for battle, General Lee was inclined to engage as soon as practicable, but did not order. All troops that he could hope to have were up except R. H. Anderson's division, which was near enough to come in when the battle was in progress. I asked him to be allowed to make a reconnoissance of the enemy's ground, and along his left. After an hour's work, mounted and afoot, under the August sun, I returned and reported adversely as to attack, especially in view of the easy approach of the troops reported at Manassas against my right in the event of severe contention. We knew of Ricketts's division in that quarter, and of a considerable force at Manassas Junction, which indicated one corps." Lee acquiesced to Longstreet's advice, which some Lost Cause advocates would later claim gave Longstreet the confidence to go against Lee's wishes. Considering Longstreet's disobedience of General Lee's wishes to be nearly insubordination, Lee's most famous biographer, Douglas Southall Freeman, later wrote: "The seeds of much of the disaster on July 2, 1863, at the Battle of Gettysburg were sown in that instant—when Lee yielded to Longstreet and Longstreet discovered that he would." However, Longstreet's men had marched about 30 miles and briefly fought at Thoroughfare Gap the day before, so Longstreet was well aware that his men were anything but fresh.

One of the sources of Longstreet's apprehension that day was Fitz-John Porter's corps, one of the few commands from the Army of the Potomac that would engage in substantial fighting during the battle. Porter, along with McDowell's corps, were on the left of the Union line and were advancing northwest toward what they thought would be Jackson's right when they encountered Stuart's cavalry. In fact, Stuart's cavalry had just escorted Longstreet's men to the field, and as they engaged in skirmishing, orders from Pope for Porter and McDowell arrived.

Porter

The orders, now known as the "Joint Order", essentially ordered Porter to perform the impossible. The order suggested that Porter and McDowell move along the Manassas-Gainesville Road (as they had been doing) toward Gainesville while also maintaining contact with the rest of the Union line, which at the time had John Reynolds's division on the left flank. At the same time, the order stated "as soon as communication is established [with the other divisions] the whole command shall halt. It may be necessary to fall back behind Bull Run to Centreville tonight." Finally, Pope's order added a caveat: "If any considerable advantages are to be gained from departing from this order it will not be strictly carried out."

Historian John J. Hennessy, who wrote a history on the campaign, has since labeled Pope's order "masterpiece of contradiction and obfuscation that would become the focal point of decades of wrangling." To start, it was not possible for this column to continue marching toward Gainesville and maintain contact with the left of the Union line at the same time. And in addition to the incredibly murky and contradictory suggestions, Pope gave the men on his left this order without realizing that Longstreet's wing of the army had arrived on the battlefield to Jackson's left, a deployment that induced Porter to widely choose not to make an attack on the 29th. Despite the wisdom of the decision, it was one that would lead to Porter being court-martialed and effectively ending his military career.

Somehow, even in the years after the Civil War, Pope remained mistaken about Longstreet's dispositions on the afternoon of the 29th, and he continued to direct his vitriol at Porter, who he believed had disobeyed his orders out of loyalty to McClellan, writing:

"From 1:30 to 4 o'clock P. M. very severe conflicts occurred repeatedly all along the line, and there was a continuous roar of artillery and small-arms, with scarcely an intermission. About two o'clock in the afternoon three discharges of artillery were heard on the extreme left of our line or right of the enemy's, and I for the moment, and naturally, believed that Porter and McDowell had reached their positions and were engaged with the enemy. I heard only three shots, and as nothing followed I was at a loss to know what had become of these corps, or what was delaying them, as before this hour they should have been, even With ordinary marching, well up on our left. Shortly afterward I received information that McDowell's corps was advancing to join the left of our line by the Sudley Springs road, and would probably be up within two hours. At 4:30 o'clock I sent a peremptory order to General Porter, who was at or near Dawkins's Branch, about four or five miles distant from my headquarters, to push forward at once into action on the enemy's right, and if possible on his rear, stating to him generally the condition of things on the field in front of me. At 5:30 o'clock, when General Porter should have been going into action in compliance with this order, I directed Heintzelman and Reno to attack the enemy's left. The attack was made promptly and with vigor and persistence, and the left of the enemy was doubled back toward his center. After a severe and bloody action of an hour Kearny forced the position on the left of the enemy and occupied the field of battle there."

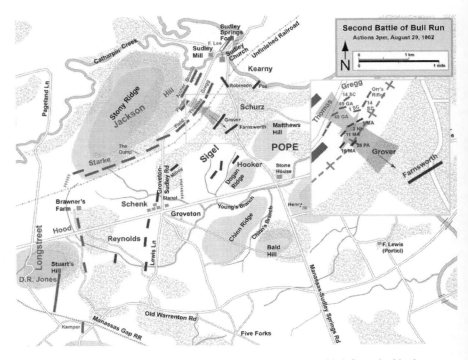

As Pope's account indicates, his failure to understand the situation on his left resulted in the mistaken belief that the afternoon would include attacks on both of Jackson's flanks instead of just one desperate assault on Jackson's left yet again. The highlight of that attack came when a brigade led by Brig. Gen. Cuvier Grover successfully marched into a gap in the Confederate line, only to be repulsed because Kearny's division did not support it. Furthermore, Pope had expected the attack to be a diversionary tactic while his left surprised Jackson's right, still unaware of Longstreet's position. Eventually Brig. Gen. Dorsey Pender's brigade sealed the gap in A.P. Hill's line.

While this was going on, Pope ordered John Reynolds to advance on the left, during which Reynolds ran into Longstreet's wing and immediately called off the advance. When Reynolds reported this to Pope, Pope refused to believe it could be Longstreet and somehow thought Reynolds had mistaken Porter's corps for Confederates. The next attack was made by Jesse Reno's division of Burnside's IX Corps, which saw one brigade attack the very center of Jackson's line without support. Once again, that attack was eventually repulsed.

With every attack having been repulsed thus far, Pope continued to hold out hope that Porter's corps would deliver him a victory, even as he remained confused as to why he hadn't heard any fighting or accounts of fighting on his left. At 4:30 p.m., Pope sent orders to Porter to attack, but Porter did not get that message until it was dusk, and he still had Longstreet in his front, making an attack on Jackson's right impossible. But Pope ordered Kearny's division to attack Jackson's left in conjunction with his order to Porter, so Kearny's division surged forward around 5:00, crashing into A.P. Hill's division, which had already taken most of the Union attacks during the day.

Kearny reported what went wrong with this new wave:

"During the first hours of combat General Birney, on tired regiments in the center falling back, of his own accord rapidly pushed across to give them a hand to raise themselves to a renewed fight. In early after noon General Pope's order, per General Roberts, was to send a pretty strong force diagonally to the front to relieve the center in the woods from pressure. Accordingly I detached for that purpose General Robinson, with his brigade; the Sixty-third Pennsylvania Volunteers, Colonel Hays; the One hundred and fifth Pennsylvania Volunteers, Captain Craig; the Twentieth Indiana, Colonel Brown, and, additionally, the Third Michigan Marksmen, under Colonel Champlin. General Robinson drove forward for several hundred yards, but the center of the main battle being shortly after driven back and out of the woods, my detachment, thus exposed, so considerably in front of all others, both flanks in air, was obliged to cease to advance, and confine themselves to holding their own. At 5 o'clock, thinking-- though at the risk of exposing my fighting line to being enfiladed--that I might drive the enemy by an unexpected attack through the woods, I brought up additionally the most of Birney's regiments---the Fourth Maine, Colonel Walker and Lieutenant-Colonel Carver: the Fortieth New York, Colonel Egan; First New York, Major Burr, and One hundred and first New York, Lieutenant-Colonel Gesner--and changed front to the left, to sweep with a rush the first line of the enemy. This was most successful. The enemy rolled up on his own right. It presaged a victory for us all. Still our force was too light. The enemy brought up rapidly heavy reserves, so that our farther progress was impeded. General Stevens came up gallantly in action to support us, but did not have the numbers."

Despite launching a fierce attack, Kearny's division could only do so much for so long until Jackson reinforced Hill's line by pulling Early's brigade from his right and sending Lawrence Branch's brigade into the fight.

Although the Union assaults had finally come to an end, Lee was still entertaining thoughts about launching an attack with Longstreet's men. Once again, Longstreet successfully argued against it, insisting that a reconnaissance and an attack in the morning was a better option. John Bell Hood's division conducted the reconnaissance in force, but nightfall brought his skirmishing with the Union left to an end.

As August 29 was drawing to a close, Pope had clearly failed to bag Jackson's wing of the army, but the battle was not a debacle either. Moreover, two of McClellan's corps from the Army of the Potomac were now nearby at Alexandria, comprising about 25,000 men. Although Pope clearly couldn't count on McClellan to actually order them forward as reinforcements anymore, he still had the option of pulling his own army back to Alexandria, uniting with McClellan's army, and then figuring out a new course of action.

Instead, Pope continued to talk himself into believing that he had Jackson on the ropes, and that Lee's army was in the process of retreating. Years later, he was still trying to justify his belief that Lee was retreating, writing:

"Every indication during the night of the 29th and up to 10 o'clock on the morning of the 30th pointed to the retreat of the enemy from our front. Paroled prisoners of our own army, taken on the evening of the 29th, who came into our lines on the morning of the 30th, reported the enemy retreating during the whole night in the direction of and along the Warrenton pike (a fact since confirmed by Longstreet's report). Generals McDowell and Heintzelman, who reconnoitered the position held by the enemy's left on the evening of the 29th, also confirmed this statement. They reported to me the evacuation of these positions by the enemy, and that there was every indication of their retreat in the direction of Gainesville. On the morning of the 30th, as may be easily believed, our troops, who had been marching and fighting almost continuously for many days, were greatly exhausted. They had had little to eat for two days, and artillery and cavalry horses had been in harness and under the saddle for ten days, and had been almost out of forage for the last two days. It may be readily imagined how little these troops, after such severe labors and hardships, were in condition for further active marching and fighting."

Given Pope's mistaken beliefs, the one man who might have been able to extricate him from the mistake he was about to make happened to be the one man least inclined to help. For several days, George McClellan had at least 25,000 men within two days' march of Pope's army, yet he continued to insist that he couldn't move toward Manassas without the necessary cavalry and artillery. Pope might not have gotten much right in his writings about the battle after the war, but he rightly ridiculed McClellan's stance:

"On the 28th I had telegraphed General Halleck our condition, and had begged of him to have rations and forage sent forward to us from Alexandria with all speed; but about daylight on the 30th I received a note from General Franklin, written by direction of General McClellan, informing me that rations and forage would be loaded into the available wagons and cars at Alexandria as soon as I should send back a cavalry escort to guard the trains. Such a letter, when we were fighting the enemy and when

Alexandria was full of troops, needs no comment. Our cavalry was well-nigh broken down completely, and certainly we were in no condition to spare troops from the front, nor could they have gone to Alexandria and returned within the time by which we must have had provisions and forage or have fallen back toward supplies; nor am I able to understand of what use cavalry could be to guard railroad trains."

Understandably, supporters of Pope and critics of McClellan would heavily criticize the inaction and accuse McClellan of intentionally making Pope's life more difficult. It seems they were right; McClellan bragged in a private letter to his wife weeks earlier, "Pope will be badly thrashed within two days & ... they will be very glad to turn over the redemption of their affairs to me. I won't undertake it unless I have full & entire control." Even as Pope was launching a series of assaults against Jackson on August 29, McClellan suggested to Lincoln that they should "leave Pope to get out of his scrape, and at once use all our means to make the capital perfectly safe."

Chapter 7: August 30

One of the most ill-conceived attacks of the entire war would be made on August 30, and one of the best executed attacks of the entire war would follow it.

On the morning of August 30, Pope held a council of war at his headquarters, where he was unmistakably informed of Longstreet's position and that Jackson's men had not moved during the night. But as it turned out, some of Longstreet's men, a division under Richard Anderson, had arrived on the field late at night and woke up to find that they were dangerously close to the Union line. With that, they countermarched to link back up with the rest of Longstreet's wing, and when Pope heard of that movement it seemed to confirm to him that the Confederates were retreating, and he even telegraphed back to Washington that "the enemy was retreating to the mountains". Thus, even though Jackson's men were still in place and Longstreet was still posted on the Union army's left with about 25,000 men, Pope remained determined to attack what he believed was a retreating Confederate army.

Around noon, Pope ordered Porter to attack once again, this time in conjunction with Hatch's division and Reynolds's division on the Union left, up the Manassas-Gainesville turnpike. On the Union right, the divisions of Ricketts, Kearny, and Hooker, all of whom had fought hard the day before, were ordered to attack as well. Pope believed he was conducting a pincers attack on a retreating Confederate army, when in fact he was about to march Porter's corps right across Longstreet's front, all but exposing the left flank of Porter's 10,000 men to Longstreet's 25,000 Confederates. And far from retreating, Lee was going about bolstering Jackson's defenses, including posting artillery that could sweep the field in Jackson's front. Lee himself could not have drawn up a more favorable plan for the Confederates than Pope had.

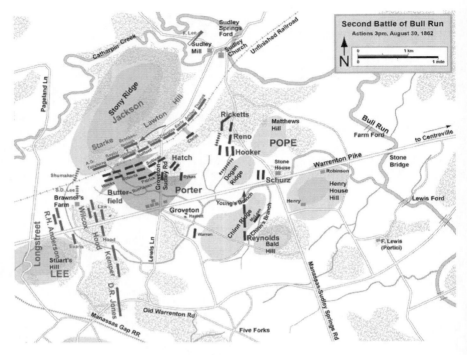

Porter's attack around 3:00 p.m.

In a campaign full of mistakes, the Union attacks managed not to be properly coordinated. Due to delays in getting his corps up, Porter would not make his assault until about an hour after the attack launched by the Union right. Jackson described how fierce the fighting was on his left in his report:

"About 2 p. m. the Federal infantry in large force advanced to the attack of our left, occupied by the division of Gen. Hill. It pressed forward, in defiance of our fatal and destructive fire, with great determination, a portion of it crossing a deep cut in the railroad track and penetrating in heavy force an interval of nearly 175 yards, which separated the right of Gregg's from the left of Thomas brigade. For a short time Gregg's brigade, on the extreme left, was isolated from the main body of the command; but the Fourteenth South Carolina Regiment, then in reserve, with the Forty-ninth Georgia, left of Col. Thomas, attacked the exultant enemy with vigor, and drove them back across the railroad track with great slaughter. Gen. McGowan reports that the opposing forces at one time delivered their volleys into each other at the distance of 10 paces. Assault after assault was made on the left, exhibiting on the part of the enemy great pertinacity and determination, but every advance was most successfully and gallantly driven back.

Gen. Hill reports that six separate and distinct assault were thus met and repulsed by his division, assisted by Hays' brigade, Col. Forno commanding.

By this time the brigade of Gen. Gregg, which from its position on the extreme left was most exposed to the enemy's attack, had nearly expended its ammunition. It had suffered severely in its men, and all its field officers except two were killed or wounded."

Porter's attack would be made under even more trying circumstances, since the division on his far left under Daniel Butterfield would have to cross about 600 yards in an open field in front of Jackson's men, who were posted behind a natural fortification in an unfinished railroad cut. On Butterfield's right was Hatch's division, which would have to march across land exposed to the batteries Lee had dutifully directed earlier in the day, not to mention Jackson's infantry. Even still, Hatch's division created a breach in Jackson's line, forcing the Stonewall Brigade to reinforce the line. The fighting was so heavy that some Confederates ran out of ammunition and began throwing rocks at the nearest Union soldiers, members of the 24th New York, which induced the Union men to throw some back.

Seeing no breakthroughs and still wary of Longstreet on his left, Porter kept his other division in reserve, but his entire command was now north of the Warrenton Turnpike and so far out in front of Longstreet that Porter's cautious alignment was still in no position to defend against the now impending flank attack. To top it off, McDowell ordered Reynolds to move his division up to support Porter's right, pulling even more Union soldiers from south of the Warrenton Turnpike and bringing them north of the Turnpike. That decision would only make it that much easier for Longstreet's assault to roll up the entire Union line, and by having only about 2,000 men still south of the Turnpike in front of Longstreet, Pope's army had inadvertently placed itself in serious danger of being trapped along Bull Run with the only roads of retreat being covered by Jackson near Sudley Springs Ford and Longstreet advancing east across the Warrenton Turnpike.

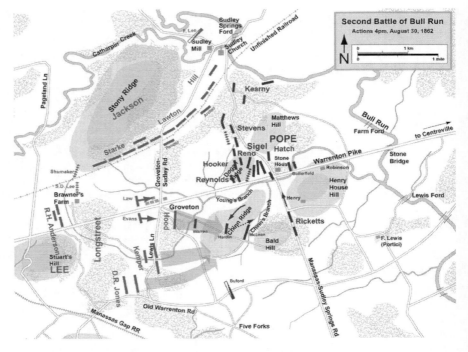

The start of Longstreet's assault at 4:00 p.m.

Around 4:00, Longstreet's assault started with the objective of reaching Henry Hill, the exact same spot McDowell's Union army had desperately sought to reach in the First Battle of Bull Run. As Longstreet explained, the advantageous positioning for his flank attack was so apparent to the men under his command that they were all but able to start the assault perfectly without even being commanded:

"Porter's masses were in almost direct line from the point at which I stood, and in enfilade fire. It was evident that they could not stand fifteen minutes under the fire of batteries planted at that point, while a division marching back and across the field to aid Jackson could not reach him in an hour, more time probably than he could stand under the heavy weights then bearing down upon him. Boldness was prudence! Prompt work by the wing and batteries could relieve the battle. Reinforcements might not be in time, so I called for my nearest batteries. Ready, anticipating call, they sprang to their places and drove at speed, saw the opportunity before it could be pointed out, and went into action. The first fire was by Chapman's battery, followed in rolling practice by Boyce's and Reilly's. Almost immediately the wounded began to drop off from Porter's ranks; the number seemed to increase with every shot; the masses began to waver, swinging back and forth, showing signs of discomfiture along the left and left centre.

In ten or fifteen minutes it crumbled into disorder and turned towards the rear. Although the batteries seemed to hasten the movements of the discomfited, the fire was less effective upon broken ranks, which gave them courage, and they made brave efforts to rally; but as the new lines formed they had to breast against Jackson's standing line, and make a new and favorable target for the batteries, which again drove them to disruption and retreat. Not satisfied, they made a third effort to rally and fight the battle through, but by that time they had fallen back far enough to open the field to the fire of S. D. Lee's artillery battalion. As the line began to take shape, this fearful fire was added to that under which they had tried so ineffectually to fight. The combination tore the line to pieces, and as it broke the third time the charge was ordered. The heavy fumes of gunpowder hanging about our ranks, as stimulating as sparkling wine, charged the atmosphere with the light and splendor of battle. Time was culminating under a flowing tide. The noble horses took the spirit of the riders sitting lightly in their saddles. As orders were given, the staff, their limbs already closed to the horses' flanks, pressed their spurs, but the electric current overleaped their speedy strides, and twenty-five thousand braves moved in line as by a single impulse. My old horse, appreciating the importance of corps headquarters, envious of the spread of his comrades as they measured the green, yet anxious to maintain his role, moved up and down his limited space in lofty bounds, resolved to cover in the air the space allotted his more fortunate comrades on the plain.

Leaving the broken ranks for Jackson, our fight was made against the lines near my front. As the plain along Hood's front was more favorable for the tread of soldiers, he was ordered, as the column of direction, to push for the plateau at the Henry House, in order to cut off retreat at the crossings by Young's Branch. Wilcox was called to support and cover Hood's left, but he lost sight of two of his brigades,--Featherston's and Pryor's, --and only gave the aid of his single brigade. Kemper and Jones were pushed on with Hood's right, Evans in Hood's direct support. The batteries were advanced as rapidly as fields were opened to them, Stribling's, J. B. Richardson's, Eshleman's, and Rogers's having fairest field for progress."

As Longstreet came crashing down from the west and south, sweeping the field before him in just 15 minutes, it became clear to Pope how tenuous his position was. Like the Confederates at First Bull Run, Pope ordered all available reinforcements to take up a defensive line on Henry Hill, and he wrote about the desperate resistance put up by some of the men under his command:

"The main attack of the enemy was made against our left, but was met with stubborn resistance by the divisions of Schenck and Reynolds, and the brigade of Milroy, who were soon reënforced on the left by Ricketts's division. The action was severe for several hours, the enemy bringing up heavy reserves and pouring mass after mass of his troops on our left. He was able also to present at least an equal force all along our line of battle. Porter's corps was halted and reformed, and as soon as it was in condition it was pushed forward to the support of our left, where it rendered distinguished service, especially the brigade of regulars under Colonel (then Lieutenant-Colonel) Buchanan.

McLean's brigade of Schenck's division, which was posted in observation on our left flank, and in support of Reynolds, became exposed to the attack of the enemy on our left when Reynolds's division was drawn back to form line to support Porter's corps, then retiring from their attack, and it was fiercely assailed by Hood and Evans, in greatly superior force. This brigade was commanded in person by General Schenck, the division commander, and fought with supreme gallantry and tenacity. The enemy's attack was repulsed several times with severe loss, but he returned again and again to the assault.

It is needless for me to describe the appearance of a man so well known to the country as General R. C. Schenck. I have only to say that a more gallant and devoted soldier never lived, and to his presence and the fearless exposure of his person during these attacks is largely due the protracted resistance made by this brigade. He fell, badly wounded, in the front of his command, and his loss was deeply felt and had a marked effect on the final result in that part of the field."

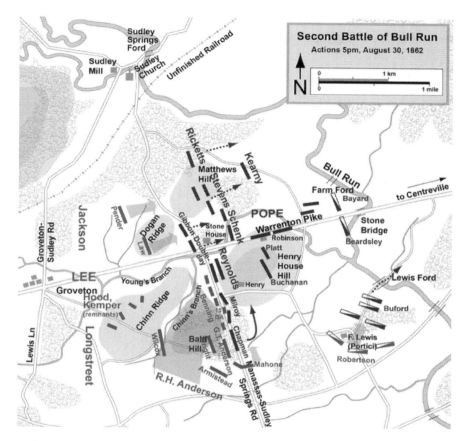

Second Battle of Bull Run
Actions 5pm, August 30, 1862

As Pope marshaled more forces into the vacuum around Henry Hill, nightfall became his best friend. By holding out on Henry Hill long enough, Pope kept the Warrenton Turnpike open so that he could retreat east across Bull Run. He was aided in this by the fact that Jackson's wing of the army was too slow to cut off that avenue of retreat, certainly a byproduct of the fact that they had been submitted to the heaviest marching and fighting of the past week. Still, Jackson has been criticized for having the slows, just like during the Seven Days' Battles; John Hennessy considered Jackson's action (or lack of it) "one of the battle's great puzzles" and "one of the most significant Confederate failures".

Though Pope's army didn't scramble back toward Washington in as much disorder as McDowell's army had during the First Battle of Bull Run, the result was ultimately the same.

And as if to antagonize Pope even more, around the same time he began retreating across the Warrenton Turnpike toward Centreville, Franklin's corps from McClellan's Army of the Potomac was marching into Centreville, about 5 miles east of Bull Run. Had Franklin been allowed to march even a day earlier, there's no telling how differently the battle might have gone.

Darkness granted Pope the respite Longstreet would not, as Longstreet noted in his memoirs: "When the last guns were fired the thickening twilight concealed the lines of friend and foe, so that the danger of friend firing against friend became imminent. The hill of the Henry House was reached in good time, but darkness coming on earlier because of thickening clouds hovering over us, and a gentle fall of rain closely following, the plateau was shut off from view, and its ascent only found by groping through the darkening rainfall. As long as the enemy held the plateau, he covered the line of retreat by the turnpike and the bridge at Young's Branch. As he retired, heavy darkness gave safe-conduct to such of his columns as could find their way through the weird mists."

The losses at the Second Battle of Bull Run were staggering, especially since the battle took place before Antietam and Gettysburg. About 10,000 soldiers, or nearly 16% of Pope's army, was killed, wounded, or captured, while Lee's army lost nearly 8,500, almost the same percentage of his forces.

Chapter 8: The Aftermath of the Battle

Lee had decisively defeated Pope, but in the immediate wake of the battle, Lee continued to hold out hope of bagging Pope's army, which he intended to accomplish by interposing his army between Pope and Washington D.C. Of course, this was made virtually impossible by elements of the Army of the Potomac, and the only major fighting after the battle came on September 1. Known as the Battle of Chantilly, Jackson's men fought some of Pope's army during a violent storm complete with lightning and pouring rain. The battle is best remembered for the death of the widely respected Phil Kearny. During the battle, Kearny, who had already lost an arm in battle, decided to investigate a gap in the Union line. When he was warned of the danger he shouted, "The Rebel bullet that can kill me has not yet been molded." Subsequently riding into Confederate troops, Kearny ignored a demand to surrender and instead attempted to escape, only to have a Rebel bullet hit him in the spine and kill him instantly. As one of the most famous soldiers of his era, Kearny was quickly recognized by A.P. Hill, who ran up to his body and yelled, "You've killed Phil Kearny, he deserved a better fate than to die in the mud."

Kearny

After two days' fighting, Lee had achieved another major victory, and he now stood unopposed in the field 12 miles away from Washington D.C. While Joseph Johnston and P.G.T. Beauregard had stayed in this position in the months after the First Battle of Bull Run, Lee determined upon a more aggressive course: taking the fight to the North. In early September, convinced that the best way to defend Richmond was to divert attention to Washington, Lee had decided to invade Maryland after obtaining Jefferson Davis's permission. In conjunction with giving Lee his approval, Davis wrote a public proclamation to the Southern people and, ostensibly, the Europeans whose recognition he hoped to gain. Recognizing the political sensitivity of appearing to invade the North instead of simply defending the home front, Davis cast the decision as one of self-defense, and that there was "no design of conquest", asserting, "We are driven to protect our own country by transferring the seat of war to that of an enemy who pursues us with a relentless and apparently aimless hostility."

Lee had also no doubt taken stock of the North's morale, both among its people and the soldiers of Pope's army and McClellan's army. In the summer of 1862, the Union had suffered more than 20,000 casualties, and Northern Democrats, who had been split into pro-war and anti-war factions from the beginning, increasingly began to question the war. As of September 1862, no progress had been made on Richmond; in fact, a Confederate army was now about to enter Maryland. And with the election of 1862 approaching, Lincoln feared the Republicans might suffer losses in the Congressional midterms that would harm the war effort.

Taking all that into account, on September 3, Lee would cross the Potomac into Maryland with his army, invading the North for the first time. Meanwhile, Lincoln restored General McClellan and removed General Pope after the second disaster at Bull Run. McClellan was still immensely popular among the Army of the Potomac, and with a mixture of men from his Army of the Potomac and Pope's Army of Virginia, he began a cautious pursuit of Lee into Maryland.

Although McClellan had largely stayed out of the political fray through 1862, McClellan's most ardent supporters could not deny that he actively worked to delay reinforcing Pope during the most recent campaign once the Army of the Potomac was evacuated from the Peninsula. Nevertheless, McClellan ultimately got what he wanted out of Pope's misfortune. Though there is some debate on the order of events that led to McClellan taking command, Lincoln ultimately restored McClellan to command, likely because McClellan was the only administrator who could reform the army quickly and efficiently.

Naturally, McClellan's ascension to command of the armies around Washington outraged the Republicans in Congress and the Lincoln Administration, some of whom had all but branded him a traitor for his inactivity in early 1862 and his poor performance on the Peninsula. This would make it all the more ironic that McClellan's campaign into Maryland during the next few weeks would bring about the release of the Emancipation Proclamation.

Of all the men who fought and died in August 1862, nobody's reputation suffered worse than John Pope, who was transferred to Minnesota to deal with the Dakota Indians, about as far away from the Civil War front as possible. Pope would spend the final 30 years of his life bitterly refighting the battle in print, as well as trying to correct the widely held opinion that he was too brash and arrogant. As he quipped in an article that appeared in the popular *Battles & Leaders of the Civil War* series, "A good deal of cheap wit has been expended upon a fanciful story that I published an order or wrote a letter or made a remark that my 'headquarters would be in the saddle.' It is an expression harmless and innocent enough, but it is even stated that it furnished General Lee with the basis for the only joke of his life. I think it due to army tradition, and to the comfort of those who have so often repeated this ancient joke in the days long before the civil war, that these later wits should not be allowed with impunity to poach on this well-tilled manor."

Not surprisingly, John Pope would continue to insist until the day he died that his detractors were mistaken, and that the Second Battle of Bull Run was greatly misunderstood:

"The battle treated of, as well as the campaign which preceded it, have been, and no doubt still are, greatly misunderstood. Probably they will remain during this generation a matter of controversy, into which personal feeling and prejudice so largely enter that dispassionate judgment cannot now be looked for. I submit this article to the public judgment with all confidence that it will be fairly considered, and as just a judgment passed upon it as is possible at this time. I well understood, as does every military man, how difficult and how thankless was the task imposed on me, and I do not hesitate to say that I would gladly have avoided it if I could have done so consistent with duty.

To confront with a small army greatly superior forces, to fight battles without the hope of victory, but only to gain time by delaying the forward movement of the enemy, is a duty the most hazardous and the most difficult that can be imposed upon any general or any army. While such operations require the highest courage and endurance on the part of the troops, they are unlikely to be understood or appreciated, and the results, however successful in view of the object aimed at, have little in them to attract public commendation or applause.

At no time could I have hoped to fight a successful battle with the superior forces of the enemy which confronted me, and which were able at any time to outflank and bear my small army to the dust. It was only by constant movement, incessant watchfulness, and hazardous skirmishes and battles, that the forces under my command were saved from destruction, and that the enemy was embarrassed and delayed in his advance until the army of General McClellan was at length assembled for the defense of Washington.

I did hope that in the course of these operations the enemy might commit some imprudence, or leave some opening of which I could take such advantage as to gain at least a partial success. This opportunity was presented by the advance of Jackson on Manassas Junction; but although the best dispositions possible in my view were made, the object was frustrated by causes which could not have been foreseen, and which perhaps are not yet completely known to the country."

Of course, it had been Pope who misunderstood the situation all along in August 1862, and it would be Pope who continued to misunderstand the campaign for the rest of his life.

Bibliography

Dawes, Rufus R. A Full Blown Yankee of the Iron Brigade: Service with the Sixth Wisconsin Volunteers. Lincoln: University of Nebraska Press, 1999.

Greene, A. Wilson. The Second Battle of Manassas. National Park Service Civil War Series. Fort Washington, PA: U.S. National Park Service and Eastern National, 2006.

Hennessy, John J. Return to Bull Run: The Campaign and Battle of Second Manassas. Norman: University of Oklahoma Press, 1993.

Herdegen, Lance J. The Men Stood Like Iron: How the Iron Brigade Won Its Name. Bloomington: Indiana University Press, 1997.

Langellier, John. Second Manassas 1862: Robert E. Lee's Greatest Victory. Oxford: Osprey

Publishing, 2002.

Longstreet, James. From Manassas to Appomattox: Memoirs of the Civil War in America. New York: Da Capo Press, 1992.

Martin, David G. The Second Bull Run Campaign: July–August 1862. New York: Da Capo Press, 1997.

Printed in Great Britain
by Amazon.co.uk, Ltd.,
Marston Gate.